Original title:
The Abominable Snowed-In Day

Copyright © 2024 Creative Arts Management OÜ
All rights reserved.

Author: Nolan Kingsley
ISBN HARDBACK: 978-9916-94-290-1
ISBN PAPERBACK: 978-9916-94-291-8

Winter's Tender Kiss

Frosty breath on window panes,
Snowmen dance in silly chains,
Sliding down the hill we go,
With mittens stuck in icy snow.

Hot cocoa spills on wooly socks,
Chasing friends in winter's mocks,
Snowball fights with giggles bright,
As snowflakes twirl in pure delight.

Footsteps in the White

Stumbling through a snowy maze,
Wondering how long this craze stays,
A squirrel laughs as I faceplant,
Oh, winter's pranks, so sly and gallant!

Tracks of mystery pave my way,
Fluffy white coats in disarray,
Puff! Puff! And plop! I'm stuck down low,
This fluffy world makes me feel slow.

A Day to Gather Dreams

Blankets piled on couches near,
Laughter echoes, spread the cheer,
Building forts, we stack them high,
With popcorn clouds that wave goodbye.

Each pillow throne a mighty seat,
Adventurers brave, no hint of defeat,
Imagined quests through snowy plains,
As outside dances winter's gains.

Heartbeats in a Snow Globe

Round and round, the flakes do swirl,
Caught up in this snowy whirl,
Bouncing off the walls of fun,
Winter's joy, oh what a run!

Inside this globe, we're free to play,
Chasing dreams on winter's sway,
Giggles trapped in frozen time,
With every chime, we feel the rhyme.

Silent Winter Serenade

Snowflakes float like silly dancers,
Chasing cats with frozen prancers.
Fluffy piles, an art of mess,
Snowmen sporting a funny dress.

Icicles ping like tiny bells,
As winter's humor surely dwells.
Hot cocoa warms our frostbit hands,
While laughter echoes through snowy lands.

The Storm's Quiet Embrace

Whirling winds with giggly tunes,
Bouncing off the stark white dunes.
Squirrels dance in fuzzy coats,
Hitch a ride on gaming goats.

Pushing snow with our bare hands,
Building forts with snowy strands.
We'll wait for spring with teasing glee,
But for now, we shout, "Snowball!" with glee.

Glacial Reflections

Mirrored ponds in icy frames,
Frogs in mittens play silly games.
Whispers float on frosty air,
As snowflakes giggle without a care.

Chill bumps dance upon our skin,
As laughter encourages us to spin.
Sliding down hills with squeals of joy,
Whirling like a mischievous toy.

Trapped Beneath the Snow

Buried deep beneath the fluff,
Tell me, have you had enough?
Sliding out of windows wide,
Hoping for a snowy slide.

Gourmet treats of snowflake pies,
Tickling noses, playful sighs.
In this white, we have some fun,
Captured hearts till winter's done.

Winter's Soft Reprieve

Snowflakes dance, quite a sight,
Kids bundle up, ready for flight.
Sleds are stacked, bright colors gleam,
Laughter echoes, a winter dream.

Hot cocoa flows, marshmallows afloat,
While dad fumbles with a funny coat.
Snowball fights cause silly slips,
As snow drifts down and winter trips.

A Still Life of Snowflakes

Outside the world is dressed in white,
Snowflakes swirl, oh what delight!
A snowman's hat is floppy and round,
As we all giggle at the ground.

Frosty noses, cheeks aglow,
Worn-out mittens, off they go.
Chasing snowballs, tripping too,
All of nature's wondrous view.

The Echoes of Snowflakes

In the quiet, whispers play,
Snowflakes fall, they laugh and sway.
A family trapped in winter's grasp,
With board games ready, no chance to clasp.

Mom's sweater's too big, dad's hat's too tight,
Socks mismatched in the soft light.
Everyone's stuck, but spirits soar,
Who knew being snowed in could be such a score?

Nature's Quiet Respite

The world is muffled, soft and bright,
Where snowmen stand, quite a sight.
Chasing each other, we slip and slide,
Through valleys of white, our laughter rides.

A snow crane's neck turns, curious and bold,
While hot soup bubbles, stories unfold.
In every flake, a giggle we find,
On this winter's day, let joy unwind.

Snowbound Dreams

Bundled up tight in fluffy layers,
Hiding from the frozen slayers.
A snowman claims my personal space,
His carrot nose, a funny face.

Hot cocoa spills as I laugh and sip,
Marshmallows floating, take a trip.
Lost mittens cause a comical fight,
Snowflakes dance in pure delight.

Chill of Solitude

Snow drifts whisper soft and slow,
No one around, just me and snow.
A squirrel winks from a frosty branch,
I think he's plotting a nature dance.

In solitude, I must confess,
My sock collection's a wondrous mess.
Stylish chaos, a fashion trend,
Who knew that warmth would need a friend?

Icicle Serenade

Icicles hanging like toothy grins,
Nature's way of showcasing wins.
Laughter echoes in the frozen air,
As I dodge the drips without a care.

Got snowballs aimed like artist's brush,
Each throw a masterpiece, a rush!
A winter's day keeps boredom at bay,
In this frosty freezer, we play!

Hibernal Sanctuary

Inside my cave of cozy bliss,
I ponder if I'll truly miss.
The world outside, all white and bright,
Meal prep? Nah, it's snack attack night!

Pajamas rule this winter scene,
No need for boots or shiny sheen.
Just me, my snacks, and a fuzzy cat,
In this hibernal haven, how 'bout that?

Tucked Beneath the Snow

Beneath the white, a world unseen,
The cat's a yeti, you've no doubt been.
With socks on hands, we start a fight,
Who'll brave the cold for a snowball's might?

The neighbor's dog, a furry beast,
Chasing flakes like it's a feast.
But when the snow drifts come too high,
We find ourselves in a snowman tie!

Stories Among the Drifts

In blizzards' clutch, we gather round,
Tell tales of heroes, lost and found.
The hot cocoa's steaming, laughter's loud,
While dad wears snow like a fluffy shroud.

A tale of squirrels stealing our bread,
A snowball battle that left us red.
With cheeks so rosy and spirits so light,
We'll brave the frost, till the morning bright.

The Art of Winter Quiet

Oh, listen close, as silence falls,
With only splatters as snowball calls.
The world's a canvas, white and pure,
Yet chaos reigns, of this I'm sure.

Sleds line up like ducks in a row,
Each rider shrieking, as fast they go.
But then, a mishap, and down they slide,
Laughter erupts, there's nowhere to hide!

In the Heart of the Storm

Outside, the wind puts on a show,
But we're all set, with snacks in tow.
Board games sprawled and laughter rings,
While outside, the cold tries to take wings.

Mom's got soup, steaming and bright,
With crusty bread, it's pure delight.
The storm might rage, but we won't budge,
Wrapped in warmth, we'll take our grudge.

Blanket of Silence

A white quilt drapes over the ground,
Hushed whispers of snow all around.
The cat pounces, slips with a meow,
As we watch comedy unfolding now.

Hot cocoa spills, a marshmallow dance,
We chuckle as we give it a chance.
Frosty windows, a silent glee,
Nature's jokes, they make us carefree.

Frost-kissed Reflections

Mirrors of ice hang from each tree,
Warblers, confused, sip tea by the lea.
The dog bounds in, all fluffy and spry,
Snowflakes tickle and make him fly.

Footprints of humor traced in the snow,
A slip here or there, a slippery show.
Giggles erupt from all near and far,
While winter reveals just how funny we are.

Sledding Into Stillness

Sleds racing down, a hilarious sight,
With each icy plunge, shrieks of delight.
We tumble and roll, like clowns in a show,
Landing in mounds of soft, fluffy snow.

The hill becomes chaos, laughter takes flight,
Each ride a treasure, purest delight.
With cheeks red and frozen, we bounce back for more,
Sending snowballs to friends with a joyful roar.

Ghosts of Winter's Past

Whispers of breezes, bring back old games,
Snowman mishaps and silly names.
Treasure hunts frozen beneath the cold haze,
Oh, how we giggle at our snowy delays!

The frost-bitten tales never seem to fade,
Chasing the shadows of fun times we made.
With each silent flurry, laughter ignites,
As we recount our frosty, comical nights.

Frosty Echoes

Snowflakes swirl like pesky flies,
Hot cocoa spills, oh what a surprise!
The cat glides by with a thunderous thump,
A snowman looms—it's just a big lump.

Sledding down the stairs, what a ride,
Landing in laundry, nowhere to hide!
Mittens mismatched, a fashion spree,
Winter's chaos, just let it be!

Chilling Silence Within

Outside, the world is a frosty sight,
Inside, we're dressed for a pillow fight.
Blankets galore, a fortress we build,
Who needs the sun when the snacks are filled?

Laughter echoes like a winter bell,
As we slip and slide, oh what the hell!
The cocoa's hot, the jokes are cold,
A day like this never gets old.

Hibernating Hearts

Beneath the covers, we snuggle tight,
Pajamas piled high, what a silly sight!
Fuzzy socks dance in a blizzard's grace,
Guess we're stuck—let's embrace the space!

Charming mugs make quite the team,
As we drift into a sugar-fueled dream.
The world outside is a chill, chill place,
But inside, oh boy, there's warmth and grace!

Winter's Dreamscape

Snowmen dance in the moonlit glow,
While squirrels plot their next big show.
Hot dogs and marshmallows, a snack brigade,
Let's build a snow fort, the best ever made!

Pillow fights erupt with laughter and glee,
As outside the mountains shout, "Let it be!"
With each cold gust, we snicker and cheer,
Embracing the fun of our snowy frontier.

Secrets of the Frosted Landscape

Snowflakes dancing, oh so spry,
Sledding penguins whoosh on by.
Hot cocoa spills, we laugh and cheer,
Winter games bring us all near.

Frosty trees wear caps so bright,
Caught a snowman in mid-flight!
He claimed he'd hide from children's glee,
But slipped on ice, oh what a spree!

Tracks of bunnies trace the hill,
While frost-cream makers laugh and thrill.
An avalanche of laughter starts,
As frozen treats fly from the carts.

So here we are, in snowy bliss,
Kissing the chill with playful wish.
Secrets hiding in every drift,
A humorous world, a frosty gift.

Whispers in a Winter Wonderland

Whispers tickle the frozen air,
Jackets tango, oh what a pair!
Snowmen chatting with silly grins,
In a world where everyone's kin.

Frosty noses, chilly feet,
Slipping together, oh what a treat!
Hats flying off in playful fights,
Caught in snowball madness of delights.

Icicles dangle, nature's prank,
Mittens missing in a snowy bank.
Laughter echoes through the trees,
As winter revels in its freeze.

So let us play in winter's game,
A funny twist, nothing the same.
Chasing joy in frosty wonder,
With whispers wrapped in snowflakes' thunder.

Winter's Whispered Embrace

A frosty hug with chilly breath,
Snowflakes pirouette, flirting with death.
We build a fort with grand design,
Hiding from snowballs, oh it's divine!

Sleds zooming down with squeaky laughs,
Hot chocolate warms our chilly halves.
Snow angels flapping, wings so wide,
Getting buried, what a hilarious ride!

Frosty critters sharing jokes,
Little froggies in cozy cloaks.
Even snowflakes, they've got style,
Twisting and spinning, all the while.

In winter's arms, we play and skate,
With laughter ringing, oh what a fate!
Embraced by cold with grins like sun,
A season with smiles, melting fun.

Frosted Retreats

In a cottage wrapped in snow,
We trade our woes for warm glow.
Winter tales and marshmallow toast,
Chasing off the winter ghost!

Frosty breath turns into clouds,
As we crack jokes, oh so loud.
Unstoppable giggles, a jolly crew,
Who knew that snow could be so blue?

Pip and Pop, the snowshoe hare,
Race through drifts without a care.
Frosted retreats, our laughter rings,
A snowy world where joy springs!

Let's build a castle, a grand affair,
With walls of snow and twinkling flare.
This frosted place, with spirit bright,
Keeps winter funny, day and night.

Flakes of Tranquility

Snowflakes tumble down with glee,
Covering the world like a soft white sea.
Sledding down the hill with laughter loud,
Why face the cold when we can be proud?

Hot cocoa spills as the mug tilts wrong,
Marshmallows jump, singing winter's song.
The cat pounces, thinking it's prey,
While I bury myself in blankets to play.

Broomsticks become our steed of choice,
Cackling like witches, we jubilantly voice.
Outside the snow, a frosty charade,
Inside, it's a circus, far from dismayed.

So here we huddle, in socks and beanies,
Sharing our tales, abstract and teeny.
When out of the chaos, a snowman's made,
With googly eyes, he'll never fade.

Frozen Adventures Await

Icicles hang like teeth of a beast,
While we bundle up for a winter feast.
On frozen ponds, we glide and slip,
Hoping our noses don't turn too blue on this trip.

An army of snowmen guards the door,
Their button eyes holding secrets galore.
With carrot noses and scarves too bright,
They watch us stumble in pure delight.

Toboggan tube races, a sight to behold,
Going faster than legends of old.
Lost in laughter, we tumble and fall,
Snowballs exchanging amidst the call.

But don't let the frostbite dance in your toes,
As we warm by the fire, exchanging our woes.
With socks kicked off and giggles untamed,
This winter adventure will be well-named.

Frosted Windows and Warm Hearts

The windows are frosted, a beautiful sight,
While inside we're warm, oh what pure delight.
The cat yawns wide, sprawled on the rug,
While we cozy up, sipping our mug.

A sprinkle of humor, a dash of cheer,
As we recount the wild times of some previous year.
Each laugh a warmth, each smile a glow,
In this cocoon of comfort, our spirits flow.

Our cheeks get rosy as we play charades,
In living room battles, no one ever fades.
With pillows as shields, we know we have won,
In this snowy embrace, life's all about fun.

So here's to the moments all frosted in white,
With friends and family, the future looks bright.
Let's float through this wonder, our hearts all aglow,
Making memories beneath the thick snow.

Solstice Stillness

A blanket of silence, the world wrapped tight,
Stars twinkle above in the chill of the night.
Winter whispers secrets to those who will hear,
As snowflakes prance, dancing without fear.

In this quiet magic, the air feels bold,
With stories to tell of the brave and the old.
We gather together, a circle of cheer,
Telling tall tales, as the holidays near.

Yet somewhere outside, mayhem unfolds,
As puppies chase snowballs, their joy uncontrolled.
With each fluffy tumble, laughter rings true,
On this still day, fun is our view.

So let's toast the season with laughs and with joy,
For even the frost can't chill the small boy.
As the night rolls onward, we'll feast and we'll play,
In the festive spirit, we'll wish it to stay.

Time Suspended in White

Snowflakes dance in the air,
Covering everything with flair.
Time seems stuck in frosty glee,
As we sip tea beneath the tree.

Sleds are flying, giggles loud,
Kids are lost among the crowd.
A snowman sporting quite a hat,
Wondering where the summer's at.

Giant boots stomp on drifts,
Delivering all winter's gifts.
Snowballs whizzing, laughter rings,
Who knew snow could give such wings!

Yet inside, the warmth persists,
Where no one ever dares to twist.
The clock ticks slow, the world at rest,
In this soft, white, timeless nest.

The Warmth Beneath the Surface

Beneath the quilt, we laugh and play,
In our cozy hideaway.
A game of cards, a snack or two,
Time drips like hot chocolate stew.

Outside the blizzard howls and moans,
But in here, we are kings and drones.
Fluffy socks and fuzzy dreams,
Embodying a life of themes.

The pets curl up to join the fun,
Purring like a cozy bun.
Snowflakes tumble, yet we stay,
Under blankets, we'll laugh all day.

A TV show and giggling fits,
Along with wild snowball skits.
Time's a trickster, oh how it flies,
In our fortress from winter skies.

Frosted Naps and Hot Cocoa

Under blankets, we snooze away,
While winter puts on its grand display.
The wind taps softly at the glass,
We just yawn and let it pass.

Choc'late marshmallows melting slow,
When outside looks like an ice cream show.
Snowmen peep through the frosty pane,
"Are you coming out?" they seem to strain.

Cranky cat in his frosty coat,
Dreams of fields that make him float.
Up and down, the snowflakes dive,
Creating laughter, keeping us alive.

A snowball battle? Please, not today!
We'll nap until the skies turn gray.
Warmed by cocoa, our spirits soar,
While outdoors, the blizzards roar.

Glimmers of Frozen Hope

Icicles glisten, like daggers bright,
A beautiful scene, yet so contrite.
As I trip on ice, I'm fully aware,
That winter's antics sometimes aren't fair.

Through the frost, the sun tries to peek,
Warming the heart, though the ground's bleak.
"New adventures await," it seems to shout,
Under snow, there's hope all about.

Laughter rings as we skate and slip,
Going for broke on this winter trip.
Each tumble, a story yet to be told,
Of frozen days, and hearts made bold.

So here we are, wrapped in our dreams,
Where everything's not what it seems.
With giggles echoing through the snow,
We remind ourselves, let's take it slow.

Serene Silence of the Snowfall

Flakes like marshmallows drift down,
Blanketing streets in a shimmering gown.
Kids outside with laughter and play,
Creating snowmen to brighten the day.

Hot cocoa waits in cups of cheer,
While outside giggles fill the sphere.
Sleds on hills go zooming fast,
Wishing this fun could forever last.

Puffs of white turn pets to fluff,
Cats in snow are soft and tough.
A snowball fight breaks out with glee,
Laughter echoing like a symphony.

As the evening falls, lights twinkle bright,
Homes cozy with warmth, a perfect sight.
Snowflakes dance off rooftops high,
Winter's joke is a cheerful lie.

Windswept Whispers

Whispers ride on the chilly breeze,
Snowflakes tickle and dance on trees.
Wind chimes jingle with a frosty laugh,
Nature's card of a silly photograph.

Frolicking squirrels with tiny feet,
Wonder if snow is a tasty treat.
Each leap a giggle, each slide a cheer,
Comical chaos that we hold dear.

With every gust, the flakes do swirl,
Dashing through, they twirl and whirl.
Covering paths, they play hide and seek,
Nature's sense of humor, oh so unique!

In the warmth, we sip and sigh,
Watching snowflakes tumble by.
As the world dons a wintery dress,
We feast on laughter, nothing less.

Amongst the Quiet Pines

Among the pines, the stillness grows,
Whispers float where no one goes.
Footprints vanish, as if to tease,
Where did we go? Who's keeping these?

Here in the snow we find delight,
Snowball battles turn into flight.
Pine cones tumble, nature's toys,
Mixing snow with giggling joys.

Around the fire, we gather tight,
Retelling tales of that day so bright.
Marshmallow roasting makes us grin,
Snow's sweet magic draws us in.

Under the stars, frosty and clear,
Echoes of laughter, memories dear.
Amidst the quiet, joy takes flight,
Winter's playtime, a pure delight!

The Poetry of Winter's Pause

In winter's pause, the world turns white,
Silence settles, a soft delight.
Jokes of snowmen, tall and round,
A funny hat or a carrot found.

Chasing dogs with wagging tails,
Disruption of snow, as laughter prevails.
Every tumble, an amusing misstep,
With fresh snow, we take our prep.

Hot pies cooling on windowsills,
As snowflakes dance, the laughter spills.
Games of charades by the warm light,
Mirth dances about, oh what a sight.

So here we sit, in joy and cheer,
Among the snow, friends gather near.
As winter whispers, we all embrace,
Finding humor in this enchanted space.

The Dance of Snowflakes

Snowflakes twirl like little clowns,
They tumble down in fluffy gowns.
With every puff, they weave and swish,
A winter show, a snowy wish.

Children cheer, their cheeks aglow,
Catch a flake and scream, "Oh no!"
Snowmen wobble, hats askew,
In this circus, laughter grew.

Sleds go flying, one by one,
Into the drifts, oh what fun!
Hot cocoa waits on the side,
As winter's mischief takes a ride.

So dance along, you cheeky flakes,
In joyful plays that winter makes.
For each soft fall is but a tease,
A playful jest, a snowy breeze.

Winter's Gracious Hold

The frost arrived with a cheeky grin,
As we all wondered where to begin.
With a quilt of white, the world now sleeps,
While inside, the laughter softly peeps.

Socks are scattered, piled high with care,
In cozy forts we giggle and share.
The ice outside gives a slippery charm,
But inside, our hearts stay warm and calm.

The kettle whistles, a bubbling song,
As we huddle close where we belong.
The frost can knock, the winds can howl,
But here in warmth, we dance and growl.

So bring on snow, let it blanket all,
We'll laugh and play, we'll never fall.
In winter's hold, our joy will stay,
Creating treasures day by day.

Cozy Corners of the Hearth

In corners quaint, the shadows play,
While wind outside does twist and sway.
The flames leap high, a merry jest,
As we toast marshmallows in our nest.

A board game sprawls across the floor,
While laughter spills, we ask for more.
Amid the chill, our spirits thrive,
In crackling warmth, we're so alive.

Cushions tossed and blankets wide,
We build our forts, we won't abide.
The chilly gusts can knock all night,
But snug inside, it feels just right.

So let the storm rage, let it compete,
We've got our jokes, our food, our heat.
In cozy corners, we'll stay and play,
While winter whispers far away.

Silent Snowfall

The world outside dons a gleaming coat,
As flakes like feathers begin to float.
In silence soft, they blanket the ground,
And all the while, we laugh around.

The crunch of boots is music sweet,
A symphony of winter's treat.
We throw our hats into the air,
And pause a moment, without a care.

The trees wear crystals, a sparkling show,
As giggles echo in the falling snow.
The quiet whispers secrets shared,
While frosty air is lightly dared.

So let the snow fall, soft and white,
In frosty frolic, it feels so right.
With every flake, another jest,
In silent wonder, we are blessed.

Embracing the Chill

Frosty fingers, toes so numb,
I tried to brew some cocoa, glum.
The cat's a snowball, fur so white,
She pounces on my face at night.

The snowdrift's high, I cannot see,
My door is blocked, oh woe is me!
I dance with squirrels on the porch,
And sing loud songs by candle torch.

My mittens stolen, where'd they go?
I thought I left them in the snow.
But with each slip and each small fall,
I laugh, I giggle, oh, what a brawl!

So let it snow, let chaos reign,
I'll toast to cabin feet in pain.
With friends inside, and laughter bright,
This winter's joy feels just so right!

Frosty Musings

Snowflakes dancing, swirling round,
I trip and land upon the ground.
The snowman's grin is wider still,
As I wave at him with a thrill.

Hot soup's a must for frosty days,
But somehow, I find funny ways.
I spill it all upon my lap,
And sit and ponder in a nap.

The dog is lost, or so it seems,
In white and fluff, he chases dreams.
He rolls and tumbles, joyous play,
While I just sip my drink today.

So here we are, all cozy tight,
With fuzzy socks and pure delight.
Let winter wrap us like a hug,
In cold, we find our warmth, so snug!

The Comfort of Snowy Embrace

Chill seeps in, but I don't mind,
With blankets piled, I'm wrapped, aligned.
My hot cocoa's got a marshmallow sea,
It floats and dances, just like me!

Outside is quiet, blanket of white,
I watch the flakes in dappled light.
A snowball fight breaks out next door,
I laugh and cheer, 'Just one more score!'

The cat's surprised by frost's soft touch,
She leaps and bounds—oh, that's too much!
Amid the bliss, my socks are wet,
But silliness is something I won't regret.

So here I stay, in winter's fold,
With stories shared and laughter bold.
Embracing joy, the chill, the fun,
Let's play all day till day is done!

Winter's Night Whispers

Moonlight glimmers on snowy lanes,
While I am bundled, lost in gains.
The world a wonder, soft and bright,
I step outside, oh what a sight!

The snowman winks with eyes of coal,
I slide on ice, I lose control.
I tumble down, then laugh it out,
With winter tales I dream about.

A snowflake lands upon my nose,
And winter's kiss, it gently shows.
With giggles shared by candle glow,
We spin our tales in swirling snow.

So let the winds howl as they may,
In cozy homes, we'll laugh and play.
With every flake that falls, we cheer,
For snowy nights bring friends so dear!

The Magic of a Frosty Escape

A blanket of white covers my street,
While penguins dance on frozen feet.
Snowballs fly, oh what a sight,
As snowmen wave, pure delight!

Hot cocoa spills, marshmallows float,
My cat dons a soft wool coat.
Sliding down hills on a lunch tray,
I laugh until I can't feel my face!

Frosty friends join to play,
In this winter wonder, we won't delay.
Snowflakes twirl, a dazzling show,
We'll sing and dance, let worries go!

As long as the snow keeps piling high,
I'll pretend to be an expert spy.
In a day full of snow, life's a game,
Wishing every winter could be the same!

Isolation in White

Trapped with cookies, oh what joy,
A hefty snowman, my favorite toy.
The world outside is a fluffy maze,
I'll nap till spring, in a snowy haze.

Pajamas on, I'm feeling bold,
In a frosty castle made of gold.
With the fridge stocked like a frozen vault,
Isolation? No, it's a frosty waltz!

I watch the world with my mug in hand,
As snowflakes pile, they make a grand stand.
My cat looks at me with confounded glee,
This blizzard made a home just for me!

When the snow plow finally arrives,
I'll hide away with all my pies.
Let the world think I've gone away,
In my snowy kingdom, I'll surely stay!

Whispers of Winter's Creatures

In the quiet, critters play,
Skiing squirrels on display!
Bunnies hop with fluffy tails,
While bears are dreaming under veils.

The owls shout tales of chilly nights,
As snowflakes twirl in twinkling lights.
A dance of shadows, laugh and shout,
Who knew winter could be so stout?

Raccoons pull pranks in the moon's soft glow,
Wearing snow hats, put on quite a show.
While deer tiptoe, all noses in air,
You can't help but giggle, it's too rare!

Nature's whimsy spins a yarn,
Where winter's critters steal the charm.
In a world so bright, nothing seems grim,
Each frosty whisper starts to brim!

A Forest in Slumber

The trees wear blankets, thick and white,
Whispers of snores fill the night.
A bear in a cave, snug as a bug,
Dreaming of honey, all warm and snug.

Tiny critters nestled in beds,
While snow drapes across their tiny heads.
A sleeping fox rests by the brook,
It's a deathly quiet, a storybook!

Snowflakes gently kiss the ground,
In this white wonder, peace is found.
Each branch bows low, heavy and proud,
While nature sleeps, oh it's quite loud!

The forest dreams of springtime joy,
Where sun will warm, and kids will toy.
But for now, in this snowy embrace,
We laugh and celebrate winter's grace!

Snowfall's Embrace

Winter's fluff spills from the sky,
Poking noses, kids run by.
Snowflakes tickle, laughter loud,
White wobbly snowmen, proudly bowed.

Hot cocoa sloshes, mugs in hand,
Sipping warmth while we all stand.
Fingers frosty, cheeks all red,
Snowball fights, we dodge instead.

Sleds on hills, a whoosh and glide,
All the pets, they pause and hide.
Worn-out boots, boots piled high,
Giggles echo, oh my, oh my!

When does spring come, we all moan,
But for now, we're stoked and prone.
Stuck inside with games and cheer,
Snowfall's hug, we hold it dear.

Absence of Footsteps

Silent streets, the world is still,
Blanketed soft, the night is chill.
No pitter-patter, kids have ceased,
Just snow angels where they've teased.

Goblins laugh in the frosted air,
Red-nosed reindeers pair and stare.
Snowman's hat flies in the breeze,
Carrot noses wave with ease.

Mismatched mittens, lost in mounds,
They vanish where snow confounds.
Blanket forts that block the cold,
Adventures start for the bold.

Tomorrow's trek may bring some fun,
But tonight, we play till we've spun.
Absence of footprints, tales unfold,
Of frozen silliness, bright and bold.

Heartbeats Beneath the Ice

Underneath a layer cold,
Warm hearts beat, brave and bold.
Jumping high on hidden lakes,
Slipping, sliding, oh, the shakes!

Chasing friends through frosty air,
Laughter bubbling everywhere.
Snowflakes kiss our rosy cheeks,
Nature's giggles, so unique!

Snowball aimed, the hit's not fair,
Wishing now for a wild dare.
Wrapped in layers, snug and tight,
We play until the morning light.

Games of chase, we spin and race,
Swaying trees softly embrace.
Heartbeats loud beneath the ice,
In this circus, oh, how nice!

Drifting Memories in White

Frosty paths, where laughs abound,
We lose our hats and boots we've found.
Cherished moments drifting slow,
In the white, we skip and flow.

Puffs of breath, like clouds in play,
Sculpting dreams in snowy sway.
Winter's magic, playful tune,
Under a soft and glowing moon.

Tales exchanged with frozen fingers,
Every gust of wind still lingers.
Slopes of joy, we race with glee,
Ev'ry snowdrift, a memory!

Winter wraps us, snug as a hug,
Built like castles, none to shrug.
Drifting hopes in snowy light,
We revel in this frosty night.

Winter's Gentle Lullaby

Snowflakes dance in swirling flight,
They tickle our noses, what a sight.
With every flake that hits the ground,
A cozy world of white is found.

Sleds are flying down the hill,
Voices echo, laughter spills.
Hot cocoa waits with marshmallow fluff,
Winter's chill may be rough, but this is fun stuff!

Frosty breath like dragons' spew,
Warming hearts in skies of blue.
We build snowmen, round and jolly,
Decked in scarves, they wave and folly.

As night falls, the stars take stage,
Chasing winter blues away, we engage.
With snowball fights, we act like kids,
In this snowy world, let laughter bid.

Quietude Wrapped in White

Fluffy pillows on the ground,
Whispers of snow without a sound.
Footprints lead to nowhere fast,
As we race to make the fun last.

Cats are leaping, dogs take flight,
Finding joy in pure delight.
Chasing tails in a snowy spree,
Winter's magic, wild and free.

Jackets zipped, we march outside,
With cheeks so rosy, we take pride.
To build a fort, a splendid view,
We giggle as snowballs soar anew.

When the sun dips, our warmth is gone,
We scurry home, a race we won.
With rosy cheeks and smiles that gleam,
In quietude, we dream a dream.

A Frosted Journey

On this path of glistening white,
Every slip brings a goofy sight.
Snowmen wave from yards so wide,
In this frosted fun, we take pride.

Hot soup bubbling, bread in tow,
Pants are soaked, but we don't know.
With every slide and winter cheer,
We're grateful for the snowy frontier.

Giant hills, oh what a thrill,
Sleds whipping fast, the air is still.
Laughter echoes, joy on display,
A frosty journey makes our day.

But at day's end, we drift away,
Cocoa dreams end this grand play.
Snowflakes twinkled under light,
In our hearts, warmth shines bright.

Unwritten Pages in Snow

Here we are, blank pages wide,
Covering the world, snow applied.
Each footstep writes a tale anew,
In this white wonder, magic grew.

A snowball zipped from friend to foe,
A winter battlefield, no time to slow.
With sticks for swords and laughter loud,
In this frozen blitz, we're so proud.

The trees stand tall in frosty coats,
Our laughter floats like playful notes.
Snow angels spread their wings in cheer,
In this white world, we hold dear.

As dusk falls, we huddle tight,
With stories spun of snowy nights.
Tomorrow's tales will surely grow,
On unwritten pages, in the snow.

Lost in the Snowy Abyss

Pants are soaked, and socks are wet,
I lost my boot, and I can't forget.
The snowman laughs, oh what a sight,
He stole my scarf, it's quite a fright.

Fluffy flakes, they twist and twirl,
My nose is red, it starts to whirl.
Every step feels like a dance,
But who knew snow could cause such a prance?

A snowball fight, we're losing fast,
My best throw lands, with a splash and blast.
But oh dear, look at that lack of aim,
I should've known I can't play this game.

Trudging home with cheeks aglow,
Chasing dreams in the winter's flow.
I fall again, I laugh and moan,
In this snowy abyss, I'm not alone.

Cocooned in the Cold

Nestled tight in blankets galore,
Watching icicles hang by the door.
I've lost my will to brave the storm,
Sock monsters are my new norm.

Hot cocoa spills, oh what a mess,
Marshmallows float, they feel so blessed.
Couch potatoes, that's our fate,
Stuck inside, well, isn't that great?

Socks mismatched, the cat's gone wild,
In the snowy cocoon, I'm just a child.
We play charades, who can pretend?
We'll keep it going till the very end.

Outside the world shivers and shakes,
But here inside, we make no mistakes.
We giggle and snort, what joy we hold,
In our little fortress of cozy and cold.

Through the Winter's Veil

Through frosty panes, we peek and stare,
What's that outside? A polar bear?
The world looks like a giant cake,
With layers of snow, we can't forsake.

I trip and fall, a signature move,
The puppy laughs, he's in the groove.
He bounds ahead with boundless glee,
As I'm tangled up like a lost tree.

Snowflakes swirl like confetti in air,
We make a snow angel, without a care.
The neighbor's cat, with cautious feet,
Turns into a furry snowball sleet.

Through winter's veil, time drips so slow,
With laughter and love, we steal the show.
A snowy escapade, oh what a thrill,
We frolic on, 'til the sun's high still.

White Dusk's Gentle Touch

Dusk settles in with a snowy hush,
The world outside is in a rush.
Sleds fly by with squeals of delight,
As I sip tea on this cozy night.

Fluffy bunnies hop without a care,
I see them munching the cold night air.
My mittens are gone, oh what a sight,
My fingers are cold, but my heart's just right.

We build a fort, a fortress grand,
With walls of snow, it's truly planned.
But oh no! It starts to cave,
As I shout, "Quick! Be a snow slave!"

With laughs and joy, we run amok,
The snowball fight turns into a rock.
White dusk wraps us in a frosty glow,
Creating memories in the winter's flow.

Snowbound Solitude

Flakes like feathers drift and swirl,
Cozy blankets in a warm, soft curl.
Socks with holes, a fashion crime,
Dancing like penguins, oh so sublime.

Chili bubbling, oh what a treat,
Snow men grinning on the street.
Frozen friends come to play,
Laughing the winter blues away.

Hot cocoa spills A frothy tide,
Snowflakes melt on my slide.
In this frosty, silly show,
I might just stay, not go, oh no!

Sledding down an icy hill,
Hopes of glory, heart a thrill.
With every tumble, giggles sound,
Joyful hearts in flakes abound.

Dreams Etched in Frost

Eager paws against the glass,
Searching for the neighbors' grass.
Squirrels scurry, hiding nuts,
While we giggle and throw snow cuts.

Shoveling paths takes us afar,
Chasing flakes, we're winter stars.
With hats askew and boots that squeak,
Playground laughter, oh so unique!

Icicles hang like nature's lance,
Within the chill, we still dance.
Each fluffy dollop, a grand surprise,
Masks of winter on squinty eyes.

Blank canvas glistening, pure white glow,
We're painting dreams with each flake's flow.
In a world of snowball throw,
Happiness in each icy blow.

The Palette of Winter's Chill

Snowy skies, a patchwork bright,
Clumps of laughter at morning light.
With rosy cheeks, we run and play,
Colorful chaos, a snowy display.

Painting snowmen, silly and stout,
Wobbling noses, no doubt about.
Frolicking friends in a flurry of fun,
Landed with laughter at every run.

Hot soup steaming, a winter feast,
Teas and tales, joy unleashed.
Frosty cheeks and a chatter so merry,
Sledding down hills, oh, how we carry!

Winter delights, oh what a thrill,
Twirling in snow without the chill.
Each flake tells a tale of delight,
In the palette of frost, we take flight.

Up with the Icicles

Icicles hanging like pointy stakes,
Kittens pouncing, making mistakes.
Snowballs fly—oh what a mess,
Giggles and stumbles, a fluffy dress.

Mittens mismatched, a fashion feat,
Waddle away with frosty feet.
Caught in the snow, a comical slide,
With each tumble, more joy to decide.

Frozen fingers wrap round hot tea,
Warmed by laughter, as silly as we.
Sneaky snowballs behind every door,
Winter's whispers, a playful lore.

With each icicle that twinks and glints,
We dive into fun, without hints.
A snow-covered world, a grand display,
Let's frolic and play, come what may!

Whiteout Chronicles

Flakes are flying, sights are blurred,
My cat's a snowball, how absurd!
Windows foggy, can't see the street,
Let's bake cookies, a cozy treat!

Sledding down the couch with flair,
Can't find my gloves; they're somewhere there!
Snowman's a cat, with a hat that's blue,
Oh, just what am I supposed to do?

Last night's dinner, now a solid block,
Lost in the fridge, time to unlock!
Binge-watching shows, my favorite game,
This weather's wacky, but who's to blame?

I'll take a nap, it's snowing wide,
Dreaming of tacos, what a ride!
Snowed in with snacks, what fun we'll find,
Tomorrow, let's see what's left behind!

Cocooned in Winter's Arms

Under blankets, nice and tight,
Sipping cocoa, feels just right.
Outside is chaos, I'll just stay,
Wrapped in warmth, come what may!

Boredom creeps, then off I go,
Crafting snowflakes, look at them glow!
Battling dust bunnies, fierce and bold,
In my home, I'm a hero, behold!

Caught in a whirl of dreams and snacks,
A fort of pillows, oh, what a lack!
Designing tunnels, from here to there,
Even the dog thinks we're quite the pair!

Here's to the fun of being stuck,
Making snow angels, oh, what luck!
Winter may rage, but we'll keep warm,
In this little haven, safe from harm!

Solace in the Snowfall

White fluffy mounds all around,
A grand soft blanket covers the ground.
With hot chocolate, I stand so proud,
Seeing my dog leap, barking loud!

Creating a kingdom of ice and cheer,
With slippery socks, I've conquered fear!
The yard's transformed, a frosty spree,
Snowball fights – now that's the key!

Tickle fights happen, laughter fills,
Nature's a prankster, throwing chills.
Inside we feast, it's cookies galore,
Maybe tomorrow, I'll brave the door!

As the wind howls, we're snug in here,
Sharing stories, joy, and cheer.
Let the world freeze, we won't budge,
In our snowy castle, we're the judge!

Ensnared by the Flurries

Flurries twirl like dancers, free,
Caught in my boots, oh woe is me!
Mittens mismatched, oh what a sight,
Chasing snowflakes, morning light.

Caught in a lurch, time's on freeze,
Now I'm inside, no chance to tease.
The fridge is bare, but I don't care,
Pizza delivery? No one's there!

With board games piled, let's make a play,
Strategy fails, I'll eat my way.
Socks and slippers, match or not,
Creating mayhem, on my spot!

As winter whirls, we dance with glee,
Forget the outside, just you and me.
In this shimmering mess, we'll be fine,
With laughter and joy, I raise my wine!

Breathe in Winter's Essence

Huddled here, with mugs in hand,
We watch the snowflakes start to land.
Outside the world, a snowy mess,
Inside, we share our warmth and zest.

The wind howls like a melodious beast,
While inside we feast like it's a grand feast.
A sock on the floor, a hat on the chair,
We laugh at the chaos, without a care.

The dog makes a dash, slips in delight,
Chasing the kids, a comical sight.
Together we tumble, we play and we shout,
This winter wonder, there's never a doubt.

Through frosty windows, we peer out wide,
At snowmen forming, with arms open wide.
Laughter erupts in this snowy spree,
As we breathe in winter's essence, carefree.

Ethereal Silence

In the stillness, snowflakes gently land,
As laughter whispers, hand-in-hand.
Sticky hands craft a snowy head,
While inside, the oven's warming bread.

The cat prances, looking quite sleek,
While kids in pajamas loudly squeak.
With every flake, a giggle begins,
As the snowman outside grows taller than sin.

The wind may whistle its winter tune,
But we dance indoors, beneath the moon.
In blankets we snuggle, making a fort,
Who knew snow days could be such a sport?

As snow settles thick on branches and cars,
We tell old tales 'neath the glow of our stars.
In this ethereal silence, laughter is bound,
With each playful moment, pure joy is found.

A Canvas of Snow

White sheets wrap the world in pure glee,
A canvas of snow, oh look at it flee!
Kids run amok, boots too big,
Making snow angels, doing a jig.

Fluffy, white laughter fills the cold air,
While dogs jump around, causing a stare.
Hot cocoa waits with marshmallows crowned,
As we relish the moments, joy unbound.

Snowball fights erupt with playful glee,
A chorus of laughter, carefree and free.
Slipping and sliding, we chase down the hill,
With every tumble, our hearts are still.

The sun may break through, with a glimmer of light,
But nothing beats snow on a playful night.
In this winter wonderland, we'll frolic and play,
A canvas of snow, let's seize the day!

Toylands and Snowmen

Toylands arise in a kingdom of white,
Creativity blooms under soft candlelight.
We build our snowmen, each one unique,
With a carrot for noses, a fashion critique.

A dollhouse is made from odds and ends,
While laughter and chaos around us transcends.
The wind plays a tune through branches and twigs,
As we twirl and skip, dancing jigs.

Hot chocolate flows like a warm river's bend,
As the world's turned to snow, let the chill end.
With cookie dough hands, we bake and we cheer,
Creating more memories, oh what a year!

In this snowy playground, dreams take their flight,
With toylands and snowmen, pure joy is in sight.
A mix of warm hearts and frosty delight,
We know in this winter, the fun feels just right.

Gathering Snowy Memories

Snowflakes tumble, swirling around,
A cocktail of laughter, we've found.
With noses red, and toes all numb,
We sip hot cocoa, oh so yum!

Laughter echoes, a playful shout,
In this white wonderland, we run about.
A snowball flies—it lands with a thud,
Our faces wear snow, a frosty mud!

With every fall, we squeal and roll,
As snow gathers high, our laughter's goal.
A sledding race down the hill we glide,
Through giggles and cheers, our joy can't hide.

When the day ends and darkness swells,
Memories spin like enchanted spells.
In this snowy magic, we'll always stay,
To cherish forever this frosty play.

Chasing Shadows in White

In the shimmer of snow, shadows creep,
We chase down giggles, no time for sleep.
With a twinkle of mischief in every leap,
Sweater fluff battles, no love for the heap!

Snowmen rise like giants, tall and proud,
Wearing our hats, the silliest crowd.
A carrot nose, but where's our stake?
We laugh 'til we cry, in the flakes we partake.

Falling flat, oh what a sight!
As icy fluff socks us left and right.
We spin and twirl in this frosty delight,
Chasing giggles, till the fall of night.

When the sun bids all of us goodbye,
We gather 'round with mugs held high.
Tales of the day warm our chilly souls,
In this snowy kingdom, we play our roles.

Fireside Chronicles

Crackling embers in the evening glow,
Stories spin fast, with a comedic flow.
From big snowballs to silly slips,
We share our fall and our crazy trips.

Hot chocolate spills and marshmallows fly,
As we roll on the floor, oh my, oh my!
With tales of snowmen that danced and pranced,
In the hearth's warm light, we laugh and glance.

Beneath the glow, hot socks on feet,
Snowy adventures that can't be beat.
A playful twist of fate we defend,
As we toast to the snow with laughter to send.

So here's to the frost, and friends all around,
In each silly saga, joy can be found.
With warmth in our hearts and giggles in air,
The fireside chronicles spark joy to share.

The Stillness of Frosted Mornings

Morning breaks soft, with silence profound,
As frost paints the world with a glittering gown.
We bundle up tight in our warm winter gear,
With a frosty goodbye, to the bed we endear.

Crunching footsteps on the fresh, white sheet,
Soundless and still, this day feels complete.
But who can resist the call of the snow?
With playful antics, we quickly bestow.

From snow angel wings to snowdrift thrills,
Each frosty moment, our laughter spills.
A teetering tower of snow banks we build,
As memories gather, our hearts get filled.

Though stillness surrounds us, we find our own way,
To dance in the flakes and seize the day.
With a wink and a chuckle, we play in delight,
In the stillness of mornings, our spirits take flight.

Frostbitten Whispers

Snowflakes dance on my nose,
While I search for some clothes.
The heater grumbles in despair,
As I flounder for a chair.

Cocoa spills on the floor,
I can't find socks anymore.
The cat laughs at my plight,
In this frosty, chilly night.

Windows fogged, I can't see,
Did I hear a snowman pee?
Blizzards howl like wild banshees,
Please send help, or at least cheese!

Stuck inside with all this frost,
I've lost my mind; it's surely tossed.
With penguins wearing my attire,
Let's hope my sanity won't tire.

Avalanche of Solitude

The snow piled high by the door,
I wonder what lies in store.
Pajamas a fluffy delight,
But they won't help me tonight.

My pants are still in the car,
What's that? Oh, a broken jar!
Socks mismatched, I start to dance,
Perhaps outside I'll take a chance.

The fridge holds little to eat,
Where's my money? I'm feeling beat.
Time for pasta, if I could find,
Some noodles left behind, so blind!

Each hour drags like a snail,
My coffee's gone—oh, what a fail!
As I entertain my own thoughts,
I guess I'll join the snowball slots.

Cabin Fever's Embrace

Here inside, the walls close tight,
Boredom creeping like a blight.
Out the window, snowflakes freeze,
A chance to tease the winter's breeze.

The microwave beeps loud and clear,
Popcorn pops, let's share a cheer.
But who will help with the crunch?
Oh wait, I've eaten the whole bunch!

Faces made in marshmallow fluff,
This hot cocoa's getting tough.
Knock, knock jokes without a pause,
Laughter erupts—yes, that's the cause!

Shelves are lined with board game dust,
We might play—but I just must,
Take a nap in this frozen den,
Tomorrow I'll start it all again.

Snowbound Reverie

Daylight breaks but feels so still,
Can't remember last night's thrill.
Breakfast is a snowman treat,
Oreo eyes and marshmallow feet.

Outside, the world looks quite absurd,
Did I hear a singing bird?
But all I see is piles of white,
What brings such strange, snowy delight?

Snowballs made with grumpy hands,
Launching at unseen lands.
The dog thinks this is all a game,
I call his name—but he feels fame.

Lost in dreams of warmer days,
Yet here, I dance in chilly plays.
Together trapped, we laugh and sing,
In this commanding, frostbite ring.

Milton Keynes UK
Ingram Content Group UK Ltd.
UKHW030750121124
451094UK00013B/823